Original title:
When I Was Me

Copyright © 2024 Swan Charm
All rights reserved.

Author: Liina Liblikas
ISBN HARDBACK: 978-9916-89-892-5
ISBN PAPERBACK: 978-9916-89-893-2
ISBN EBOOK: 978-9916-89-894-9

Beneath the Celestial Veil

In quiet realms where shadows sway,
I seek the light that guides my way.
The stars above, they softly gleam,
Whispering truths of a holy dream.

A tapestry of night unfolds,
With threads of faith in silken molds.
Each heartbeat echoes prayers of old,
Beneath the veil of mysteries untold.

In the Temple of My Essence

Within my heart, a sacred place,
Where spirit breathes in quiet grace.
Each thought a prayer that softly weaves,
A tapestry of hope that never leaves.

The walls resound with ancient cries,
A chorus of the wise and shy.
In solitude, I find my stone,
A temple built of flesh and bone.

Whispers from the Divine Within

In silence deep, the echoes ring,
A gentle touch of sacred spring.
The voice of God in every sigh,
A whisper soft, a fervent cry.

In the stillness of dawn's embrace,
I find my truth, I seek my place.
With every breath, I draw Him near,
The Divine within, forever clear.

The Fragmented Prayer

In pieces scattered, faith remains,
A broken song that yet sustains.
Each shard of doubt, a path to grace,
In every fragment, His warm embrace.

Through trials faced on shadowed roads,
I carry forth my heavy loads.
With every tear, a seed is sown,
In fragmented prayer, I am not alone.

Lost Pearls of My Spirit

In the depths of silence, I seek,
Whispers of faith, forever meek.
Once vibrant pearls, now scattered wide,
In shadows of doubt, they choose to hide.

Each tear a treasure, each sigh a prayer,
Echoes of longing fill the air.
With hands uplifted, I call their names,
Reviving the light, igniting the flames.

Through valleys of sorrow, my heart does roam,
Searching for solace, a way back home.
The weight of the world lays heavy on me,
Yet hope is a wave that sets the soul free.

As dawn breaks gently, the darkness fades,
Revealing the beauty, the grace that pervades.
With each lost pearl returned to my hand,
I dance in the love of the Holy Land.

In unity, I gather my shards,
Embracing the pain, the love, the scars.
For every lost moment, a lesson anew,
In the ocean of spirit, I find my true view.

A Journey to the Heart of Innocence

In the meadow where wildflowers bloom,
I seek the essence that banishes gloom.
With footsteps light on the path of grace,
I search for the heart, the sacred place.

The laughter of children, a melody sweet,
Guides my spirit, where love and joy meet.
In their gentle gaze, the world feels right,
A reflection divine in the young light.

With each tender whisper, I shed my fears,
As innocence wraps me, dissolving the years.
The sun sets softly, painting the skies,
A canvas of peace, where hope never dies.

Through valleys of doubt, I wander bold,
In search of the truths that were once foretold.
A journey within, as the stars align,
To find the pure heart, forever divine.

In the silence of night, I hear the call,
Of love that transcends, embracing us all.
A journey to innocence, pure and bright,
Guided by faith, through the veil of light.

The Sacred Archive Within

In the chambers of spirit, knowledge resides,
A sacred archive where truth never hides.
Each parchment of prayer, each scroll of grace,
Holds stories of mercy in a timeless space.

With wisdom as lantern, I light the way,
Through shadows of doubt that often sway.
The echoes of ancient, guiding my soul,
In the refuge of stillness, I become whole.

Pages unfold with the love of the sage,
Each word a blessing, a turning page.
Within this archive, I find my song,
A hymn for the weary, a bond that is strong.

As I wander the hallways of thought,
I gather the lessons that life has taught.
Embracing each chapter, both bitter and sweet,
In the sacred archive, my heart finds its beat.

With every reflection, the spirit ascends,
In unity wrapped, where the journey never ends.
The sacred archive, a treasure trove,
In its depths, I discover the love I once wove.

Chronicles of the Heart's Awakening

In the stillness of dawn's embrace,
Whispers of love begin the chase.
Awakened spirit, rise and sway,
To the light that guides the way.

Hope blooms under the endless skies,
Faith rekindles where sorrow lies.
Each heartbeat sings a sacred song,
United in where we all belong.

Through trials faced, we seek the grace,
A dance of souls, a warm embrace.
In quiet whispers, truth unfolds,
As ancient stories softly told.

With every tear that falls like rain,
We find our peace amidst the pain.
In every struggle, every fight,
Our hearts ignite with holy light.

Reflections on the Sacred Path

Walking gently on sacred ground,
In silence, the truth is found.
With open hearts, we take a stand,
Guided by a divine hand.

In the shadows, hope takes flight,
Illuminated by love's light.
With faith as our steadfast guide,
Together, we shall not divide.

Every step, a prayer we weave,
In every breath, we truly believe.
The sacred path, both wide and narrow,
Leads us to a bright tomorrow.

Through mountains high and valleys low,
The seeds of kindness we shall sow.
Embracing each twist and turn,
For wisdom's flame, we yearn to learn.

The Language of Lost Years

In the echoes of time, we find our tune,
Words unspoken beneath the moon.
Memories linger, softly fade,
In the silence, a serenade.

Each moment cherished, woven tight,
In the tapestry of day and night.
Lessons learned through joy and tears,
Etched in the language of lost years.

With every heartbeat, a quest for peace,
Seeking solace, a sweet release.
In the stories that we share,
Love's gentle touch is always there.

So let us gather, hand in hand,
In unity, let us stand.
For in our hearts, the truth appears,
Tenfold in the language of lost years.

Embers of Faith and Memory

In the glow of the evening fire,
Embers whisper of our desire.
Through shadows cast, and tales retold,
Faith ignites like burning coal.

Winds of change may rustle through,
Yet in the hearth, our spirits crew.
Each flicker dances to the beat,
Of memories sweet, where past and meet.

In the warmth of shared embrace,
Knowledge blooms in this sacred space.
Through trials faced, and burdens borne,
In twilight's grace, we are reborn.

With fervent hearts, we shall aspire,
To lift each other, to reach higher.
For faith remains a guiding light,
Embers glowing through the night.

Moments Cloaked in Divinity

In quiet hours, I breathe the light,
All around me, shadows take flight.
Whispers of grace fill the air,
In sacred moments, souls lay bare.

A gentle touch upon my heart,
Each prayer a map, a work of art.
Humbled by love, the divine embrace,
Guiding me softly through time and space.

Stars above, a celestial choir,
Their melodies spark an inner fire.
In stillness, I find my way back,
To the source of joy, nothing I lack.

Every tear holds a lesson dear,
In trials, there lies no fear.
With faith as my lantern in the night,
I walk the path, toward the light.

Moments cloaked in divine grace,
Reveal the truth, in every place.
With open heart, I seek to see,
The beauty in life, eternally.

A Journey Through Forgotten Paths

Ancient trails beneath my feet,
Each step reveals the bittersweet.
Echoes of prayers, lost in time,
Calling me back to rhythms sublime.

With every dawn, I seek the muse,
In nature's arms, I choose to lose.
The weight of doubt, I cast aside,
On this journey, faith's my guide.

Sunsets paint the skies with gold,
Whispers of stories yet untold.
In silence, I feel the presence near,
A gentle hand, my spirit's cheer.

Mountains rise, in splendor vast,
Each summit reached, shadows cast.
Through valleys deep and rivers wide,
I walk with love, my soul's true guide.

A journey vast, with lessons learned,
Through sacred paths, my heart has turned.
With every breath, I rise anew,
In forgotten paths, I'm born anew.

Reclaiming My Spiritual Essence

In the mirror of dawn's first light,
I find reflections, pure and bright.
The essence of my soul laid bare,
In every heartbeat, a whispered prayer.

Fragments lost in the winds of time,
Now gathered back, in sacred rhyme.
Restoring what was once in flight,
Reclaiming faith, I rise to write.

With each new step, the ground feels warm,
In the embrace of spirit's charm.
I gather words like autumn leaves,
Each one a story that believes.

Shadows may linger, yet I stand tall,
In love's reflection, I can't fall.
The essence flows, a river divine,
In every moment, I realign.

Reclaiming all that is truly mine,
In the dance of life, I intertwine.
With courage fierce, I seek the way,
To my essence, I shall stay.

The Harmonics of My Spirit's Journey

In symphonies of light and grace,
I tune my heart to a higher place.
Each note a prayer, resonant and clear,
Guiding my spirit, drawing me near.

The winds of change sing soft and low,
Beyond the veils, the soul will grow.
In every challenge, a lesson's found,
In this journey, wisdom abounds.

With every heartbeat's sacred drum,
The universe speaks, and I succumb.
To harmonies that lift my soul,
In this grand dance, I feel whole.

Beneath the stars, I find my tune,
In moonlit nights, my heart's attune.
Each moment crafted with divine hands,
In love's embrace, my spirit stands.

The harmonics of my journey sway,
A melody that lights the way.
In every breath, the truth is sung,
In the symphony of life, I'm forever young.

The Altar of Forgotten Days

In shadows cast by ancient stones,
We gather thoughts of those long gone.
Their whispers echo through the night,
A call to heart, a beckoning light.

With trembling hands, we kneel in prayer,
Offering words lost in despair.
A flame ignites from fractured past,
Illuminating paths that hold us fast.

Each tear a seed, each prayer a plea,
A bridge to realms where spirits flee.
In solemn silence, we seek to find,
The echoes of love, the ties that bind.

The altar stands, a sacred place,
Where time suspends, and souls embrace.
We honor the moments carved in clay,
As dust of ages softly lay.

Amidst the ruins, hope shall rise,
In every heart, where sorrow lies.
Through every dawn, we seek to mend,
The sacred tale that will not end.

Beneath the Cloak of Innocence

In morning light, the joy unfolds,
Childlike laughter, pure and bold.
A spirit thrives, untouched by pain,
In innocence, we find our gain.

The world may whisper words of doubt,
Yet within, love's echo shouts.
Beneath the cloak that shields the heart,
We dance, we dream, we play our part.

With every step, a prayer takes flight,
A yearning soul, embraced by light.
In grace, we walk, through storms and strife,
Finding peace, the breath of life.

A fleeting glance, a kindred smile,
Unveils the truth beneath the guile.
In timeless moments, truth revealed,
Our spirits fly, our wounds are healed.

So let us roam, our hearts so free,
Beneath the cloak, where we can see.
In every child, the world anew,
A sacred bond, forever true.

Divine Remembrances

Through prayers of old, the voices rise,
A symphony that never dies.
Each memory woven, a golden thread,
In the tapestry of all who've led.

Beneath the sky, the stars align,
In every heart, the spark divine.
We gather strength from those before,
In every smile, their light we store.

With rugged hands, we build anew,
A legacy of faith so true.
In whispered dreams, the past enshrined,
In love's embrace, our souls intertwined.

Through trials faced, and battles won,
In sacred spaces, we are one.
Each shared moment, a candle's glow,
Illuminating paths we know.

So raise your voice, let praises ring,
For in remembrance, we take wing.
In unity, our spirits soar,
To honor those who went before.

Revelations in the Quiet

In stillness wraps the heart so wise,
Where deeper truths begin to rise.
Through silent whispers, grace descends,
In quietude, our spirit mends.

Beneath the stars, the world unfolds,
In sacred hush, a love untold.
The heart perceives what eyes can't see,
In moments hushed, we come to be.

With gentle breath, we find our way,
In nature's stillness, we shall pray.
Each leaf that falls, a lesson shared,
In every pause, divinely aired.

Through trials faced, the quiet speaks,
With whispered care, the spirit seeks.
Amidst the noise, we seek the calm,
In every heartbeat, lies the psalm.

So let us linger, find the grace,
In quiet moments, we embrace.
Revelations flow like rivers wide,
In stillness, faith shall be our guide.

A Lamentation of Wandering Souls

In shadows deep, the lost ones roam,
Seeking light to guide them home.
With hearts afire, they call and plead,
For mercy's hand, in their time of need.

Through valleys wide, where sorrow reigns,
Each step they take, their burden pains.
Yet whispers soft, from spirits near,
Offer solace, calms their fear.

The path is long, the night is cold,
But love remains, more precious than gold.
In every tear, a story flows,
Of faith unbroken, a seed that grows.

With every breath, a prayer ascends,
To the heavens high, where hope transcends.
Through trials faced and battles fought,
A strength within, forever sought.

So let them wander, let them find,
The sacred truths that bind mankind.
For in the dark, a light will gleam,
Guiding souls towards the dream.

Mirrors of the Eternal

In the stillness, reflections gleam,
Echoes of a forgotten dream.
Within the heart, a spark ignites,
Illuminates the sacred sights.

Gaze into the depths, see your soul,
A journey vast, to make you whole.
Each fracture bears a tale to tell,
Of love and loss, of heaven and hell.

The cosmos sings a lullaby,
Reminding us, we cannot die.
For every ending, a new start,
In the mirror lies the sacred art.

Beneath the stars, we find our place,
In the vastness of time and space.
Together we rise, together we fall,
One spirit binds us, uniting all.

In every tear, a lesson shown,
The light in dark, the love we've known.
So lift your gaze, embrace the light,
For in your heart, the divine ignites.

In the Silence of the Sacred

In quiet hush, the world stands still,
Where time bends and hearts fulfill.
In sacred space, the spirit soars,
Whispers of love behind closed doors.

The gentle breeze, a soft caress,
Brings forth peace and divine rest.
In moments lost, we find the grace,
A sanctuary, our holy place.

With every breath, we tune our song,
In unity, where we belong.
Voices quiet, yet loud in soul,
In silence, we become whole.

Let your heart beat in rhythm true,
To the sacred pulse that lives in you.
For in the silence, wisdom grows,
In stillness, the spirit flows.

So find that pause, embrace the peace,
In sacred silence, let worries cease.
For in the dark, the stars will shine,
In the sacred space, we are divine.

The Hymn of Who I Was

In the tapestry of time I weave,
The echoes of all I believe.
A chorus sung in hues of past,
Each note a testament that lasts.

With every heartbeat, stories flow,
Memories cherished, lessons grow.
A journey forged through trials faced,
In hopes renewed, my spirit graced.

The child I was, with dreams so bright,
Wandered through the shadows of night.
Yet in the dawn, a truth emerged,
In every loss, my heart surged.

From ashes rise, transformed and bold,
A hymn of courage, a spirit of gold.
With every scar, a mark of love,
A blessing sent from above.

So sing the song of all you are,
Embrace the light, a guiding star.
For in the hymn of who I was,
Lies the whisper, the sacred cause.

Threads of Celestial Questions

In the silence of the night, we ponder,
Stars whisper secrets from afar.
What lies beyond the firmament's border?
Is solace found in the morning star?

Hearts yearn for truths only felt,
In shadows where our doubts retreat.
The sacred word, our spirits melt,
To weave the fabric of our fate.

Glimmers of faith in each breath drawn,
A quest for light in a world of gray.
With every dawn, new hopes are born,
Threads of wisdom guide our way.

In prayerful whispers, we seek to find,
The meaning etched in the skies above.
Each question a spark, igniting the mind,
Threads of love that bind us in love.

Together we rise, on wings of grace,
Embracing the path that the heart unveils.
Through trials faced, we find our place,
In the dance of creation, the spirit sails.

The Parable of the Heart's Desire

Once a seed within the heart did grow,
A yearning deep for a love divine.
In darkness, it struggles, seeking to glow,
Like vines that twist, in perfect design.

In silence, it knows what it longs to hold,
A promise whispered, sweet and rare.
With every tear, the truth unfolds,
The heart's desire, a sacred prayer.

As dawn breaks wide, we stand anew,
Embracing fate with open arms.
The tender light brings hopes in view,
Our spirits dance, undone by charms.

In the journey of faith, we find our way,
Through valleys deep and mountains high.
Each step a testament, come what may,
Bathed in the love that cannot die.

Thus we learn that love's embrace,
Is where all dreams shall find their way.
In the heart's parable, time and space,
Melt into one, with each new day.

Ascension of Forgotten Dreams

In twilight's glow, we gather near,
To share the tales of dreams long lost.
Whispers of hope, they draw us here,
Awakening visions, despite the cost.

From ashes rise, like phoenix re-born,
Forgotten ambitions seek the light.
Through trials faced and hearts so torn,
They soar again, taking flight.

Each heart a vessel, longing for more,
In the silence, our spirits cry.
Though journeys long may leave us sore,
The stars remind us how to fly.

In the tapestry of time, we weave,
Threads of moments, both bitter and sweet.
For in the dreams we dare believe,
Ascension calls, our souls complete.

With open eyes, we see the path,
To grace beyond our wildest schemes.
Together we rise from love's true bath,
Embracing the echo of our dreams.

Chronicles in the Heavenly Library

In the library of the skies, we find,
Volumes of wisdom, truths to seek.
Each page a story, gently aligned,
The essence of faith, both bold and meek.

The scribes of old, with ink of stars,
Pen tales of love, of loss, of grace.
From near and far, through endless hours,
These chronicles weave the sacred space.

What lessons lie beneath the fold?
In every tear and every laugh.
The heart inscribes what dreams behold,
In the margins, we find God's path.

With every turn of history's page,
A revelation waits, bright and clear.
In every heart, the timeless gauge,
A bridge to heaven, drawing near.

So come and read, with humble hearts,
In this sacred space, we all belong.
For in these tales, the soul imparts,
The timeless truth of life's great song.

Voices from the Wilderness

In silence, whispers call my name,
From the depths of ancient trees.
Echoes of a sacred flame,
Remind my heart, bring me to my knees.

The wind carries stories untold,
Of wanderers lost in the night.
Their courage, a tapestry bold,
Guiding souls with gentle light.

Stars above gaze with wise eyes,
Witnesses of trials long endured.
In darkness, they paint the skies,
With hope that forever is assured.

Each footstep on this hallowed ground,
Is a prayer, a vow, a grace.
In nature's arms, I am found,
Awakened to my rightful place.

The wilderness speaks, I hear its tone,
A symphony of creation's breath.
In solitude, I am not alone,
For in diversity, life finds depth.

The Temple of My Youth

Within the walls of tender days,
Where laughter danced like sunlight beams.
My spirit soared on whispered rays,
In a realm woven with dreams.

Each echo holds a sacred sound,
The joyful hearts that came before.
In fleeting moments, love was found,
Now etched upon my very core.

Petals scattered on the ground,
Memories bloom in gentle sighs.
My heart, a temple, safe and sound,
Where innocence forever lies.

Through time's embrace, I wander back,
To lessons learned in childhood's light.
In every crack, a hidden track,
Of grace that guides me through the night.

So let me cherish every stone,
Carved with wisdom from above.
In this temple, I am home,
Cradled by grace, wrapped in love.

Blessed Reminiscence

In shadows cast by fading days,
I find the blessings gently weave.
Threads of joy in life's complex maze,
Each moment shared, a heart's reprieve.

The laughter of friends, a sweet refrain,
Resonating through the halls of time.
In sorrow and joy, they spark a flame,
A melody in every rhyme.

Lessons linger, soft and clear,
In the echoes of long-lost songs.
With each reflection, I draw near,
To wisdom that forever belongs.

Gratitude transforms the past,
As I gather fragments of the whole.
In blessed reminiscence, steadfast,
I nurture the garden of my soul.

Faith whispers softly in the night,
Reminding me of love's embrace.
With open heart and steady sight,
I journey onward, filled with grace.

Parables of My Forgotten Self

In quietude, I hear the call,
Of parables lost in my mind.
Each story an echo, a silent thrall,
Revealing wisdom that I must find.

The child within, with eyes so bright,
Holds secrets wrapped in cherished dreams.
Through shadows, I seek the guiding light,
To uncover what truly redeems.

In the stillness, fear takes flight,
As I thread through memories like lace.
There lies the spark, a radiant sight,
Of a spirit yearning for grace.

Each parable speaks of love and pain,
Lessons taught by life's gentle hand.
In the tapestry of joy and strain,
I learn to rise, to understand.

So I gather fragments of my soul,
Embrace the stories left to tell.
For in these tales, I am made whole,
In the shadows of my forgotten self.

Beneath the Surface of My Being

In silent depths my spirit dwells,
Where whispers of the heart are felt.
The sacred light within me swells,
A pathway where the soul is dealt.

Within the chambers of the night,
My faith ignites a steady flame.
Unseen forces guide my sight,
A call to love, a holy name.

Through trials fierce, I seek the dawn,
The hidden truths of grace unfold.
A tapestry where hope is drawn,
In every thread, a story told.

With every breath, I rise anew,
Embraced by arms of purest light.
In depths unseen, I follow through,
To find my peace in endless flight.

In quietude, a prayer takes form,
To understand this blessed tome.
In every storm, I find the warm,
The refuge that calls my heart home.

The Revelation of Hidden Grace

In shadows cast by ancient trees,
The gentle winds of faith arise.
Through whispered words, my spirit sees,
The hidden grace beneath the skies.

Each moment holds a sacred space,
Where love flows like a river's course.
I journey forth to seek that place,
An ever-present, guiding force.

In stillness lies the grand reveal,
The secrets wrapped in tender light.
With open heart, I start to feel,
The love that banishes the night.

Beyond the veil, my soul takes flight,
With courage found in sacred song.
Each step I take reveals the bright,
Divine embrace where I belong.

In every trial, grace stands near,
A compass pointing to the truth.
As doubts dissolve, I find no fear,
For hidden grace restores my youth.

The Prayer Room of the Past

In quiet corners of my soul,
Reside the prayers of yesteryear.
With every tear, a whisper's goal,
To find the presence ever near.

The echoes of my heart still sing,
In chambers where reflections blend.
Through time I seek what love can bring,
To heal the wounds that never end.

With every word, the spirit stirs,
A tapestry of faith unfolds.
In sacred silence, the heart purrs,
A bond with grace that still holds.

The lessons learned in shadows gone,
Illuminate the sacred way.
Through trials faced, I carry on,
A prayerful heart will always stay.

In stillness found, I face my past,
Each memory a prayer in grace.
A journey long, yet meant to last,
The prayer room, my sacred space.

Sanctified Shadows

In twilight's hush, the shadows dance,
A graceful waltz of light and dark.
In every moment, sacred chance,
To find the truth, to leave a mark.

The whispers of the night confer,
On paths where faith and doubt entwine.
With every breath, my spirit stirs,
To seek the holy, pure design.

Sanctified by love's embrace,
These shadows bend, they do not break.
In every line, I see His trace,
The guiding hand in each heartache.

Through trials faced, I stand my ground,
With courage born of endless grace.
In shadows deep, my hope is found,
In every challenge, I find place.

In worship soft, my spirit glows,
The light within will always shine.
Through sanctified shadows, love flows,
A testament that life aligns.

The Resurrection of My Essence

In the quiet hush of dawn,
Hope rises with the sun,
A spirit born anew shall sing,
Old battles lost, new victories won.

From shadows deep, I emerge bright,
Revived by the grace of divine light,
Through trials faced and tears cried,
I find the strength that's ever inside.

Faith's armor wrapped around my soul,
In every crack, the light makes whole,
With lifted heart, I walk anew,
The path of love, forever true.

The echoes of despair are past,
In divine arms, my peace holds fast,
A rebirth blessed, a journey bold,
In sacred trust, the truth unfolds.

Oh, how my essence starts to soar,
Through trials faced, I seek and explore,
With spirits high, I rise and stand,
In the light of love, my heart expands.

The Sacred Journey Within

In stillness lies the sacred place,
Where whispers of the heart embrace,
A journey deep, a quest for light,
In the silent void of darkest night.

With every step, old fears may fade,
In the shadowed paths, I'm unafraid,
With trust in grace that guides my way,
The soul's pure song shall softly sway.

In meditation's tender grace,
I find my spirit's gentle space,
Lifted by love that knows no bounds,
In every silence, truth resounds.

The mirror shows reflections clear,
A tapestry of hope and fear,
Within this heart, a flame ignites,
To celebrate the spirit's flights.

The sacred journey, an inner dance,
Where love and wisdom find their chance,
In the depths of my being, I see,
The light of truth, it shines in me.

Illuminated By My Sorrows

In the depths of sorrow's tide,
I find the light that will not hide,
Each tear becomes a sacred spark,
Illuminating paths through dark.

For in the pain, the truth is shown,
With every heartache, I've brightly grown,
A canvas painted by a tender hand,
Blessed by trials, I boldly stand.

In the hollow ache, I feel the grace,
Of healing whispers, sweet embrace,
The weight of grief, a sacred song,
Transforming me where I belong.

The shadows dance, but do not stay,
In sorrow's lessons, I find my way,
Each burden bears a hidden gift,
A chance to rise, a spirit lift.

In heart's compassion, I shall rejoice,
For every struggle, I hear the voice,
That sings of hope, forever near,
Illuminated by all I hold dear.

The Lament of a Faded Spirit

Once bright and bold, I wandered free,
Now shadows linger close to me,
With whispers lost in silent nights,
I search for hope, for guiding lights.

The echoes of laughter fade away,
In memories of a brighter day,
Yet deep within, the pulse remains,
A saddened heart that still contains.

In the forest of forgotten dreams,
Amidst the flow of quiet streams,
I seek the path where joy took flight,
In the deepest dark, I crave the light.

Each sigh a prayer to heal my soul,
In the depths where shadows take their toll,
With faith, I gather every thread,
To weave the dreams that once had fled.

Though faded now, the spirit's flame,
Still flickers soft, yet knows my name,
Through every sorrow, strength I gain,
In love's embrace, I rise again.

The Rebirth of Faithful Memories

In the shadow of ancient trees,
Whispers call from days of yore,
Echoes sweet of love and grace,
Filling hearts with hope once more.

Sacred tales from life's long threads,
Gathered 'round the light of dawn,
Brimming with the warmth of souls,
Who journey on till night is gone.

With every prayer, a seed is sown,
In the garden of the mind,
Where faithful memories bloom anew,
Eternal bonds we love to find.

Through trials faced, we find our strength,
In healing words, our spirits lift,
For in the heart, the truth remains,
A wondrous, everlasting gift.

Mending the Past with Prayer

Upon the altar of our grief,
We lay our burdens, heavy stones,
In whispered prayers, we seek relief,
To heal the wounds, the broken bones.

Each tear a token of lost time,
Each sigh a plea for brighter days,
With faith, we stitch the seams of hope,
Creating light from shadowed ways.

Forgiveness flows like rivers wide,
Washing over memories fraught,
In sacred spaces, love abides,
Transforming all that pain has taught.

Let gratitude replace the blame,
As we embrace what lies ahead,
For through our trials, we proclaim,
In prayer, the past's alive, not dead.

The Resurrection of Forgotten Joy

In the quiet of a gentle morn,
Joy awakens from its sleep,
Like flowers bold, in fields reborn,
In hearts where cherished memories leap.

With every sunrise, hope reborn,
A symphony of laughter, sweet,
Unfurling petals, softly worn,
As life's rhythms twirl and meet.

Together we remember days,
When laughter danced on golden beams,
And faith lit paths in myriad ways,
Stirring dreams from restless dreams.

Now let us raise our voices high,
In celebration of the light,
Accepting joy as a gift, a sigh,
Restoring peace within the night.

A Solitary Pilgrim's Return

Upon the road, both long and true,
A pilgrim walks with weary feet,
Returning home to joys once knew,
In silence, prayers and heartbeats meet.

The stars above begin to shine,
Reflecting hopes of nights before,
Each step a vow, a sacred sign,
That love endures forevermore.

Through valleys deep and mountains high,
In solitude, the spirit grows,
For in the stillness of the sky,
The path reveals what kindness sows.

With every mile, the past transformed,
Each memory a guiding light,
In prayerful peace, the heart is warmed,
As faith ignites the endless night.

The Godly Intersection of Memory

In shadows deep where whispers lay,
The echoes of the past do pray.
A tapestry of grace adorned,
With threads of love, our hearts are worn.

Beneath the stars, our minds do roam,
To sacred realms that call us home.
Each step we take, a guiding hand,
In memories, our souls will stand.

The light of faith, a beacon bright,
Illuminates the darkest night.
Through trials faced, we rise anew,
In God's embrace, we find our view.

The pains of yore, the joys we keep,
In silence shared, our spirits leap.
We walk the path of those who trod,
At memory's gate, we meet our God.

So let us honor every thread,
The stories lived and words once said.
For in this dance of time and space,
We find the warmth of God's own grace.

Where Faith Meets Reflection

In the stillness of the morn,
Where hearts are light and souls reborn,
We pause to dream 'neath heaven's dome,
In faith, we find our sacred home.

Each thought a seed, in silence sown,
In quietude, our spirits grown.
We seek the truth in every prayer,
In moments hushed, we feel Him near.

The mirror shows the soul's intent,
Each flaw and gift, an ornament.
In faith's embrace, our flaws refine,
In reflection's depth, His light will shine.

With every breath, we strive to learn,
And from our hearts, His love we yearn.
In shadows cast by doubt and fear,
We turn to Him, for He is here.

Thus may we walk, our journey blessed,
With faith and love, our hearts at rest.
In faithful steps, we venture forth,
To find our place, our truest worth.

The Divine Call of Yesteryears

From ancient days, the stories rise,
In humble faith, beneath the skies.
Each echo sings of hope restored,
In sacred texts, a life adored.

Whispers of prophets, voices clear,
A call to hearts that still can hear.
In every trial, a lesson gleams,
A path revealed in prayerful dreams.

Through trials deep and storms of night,
The soul remembers what is right.
Each heartbeat drummed in faith's refrain,
A legacy that will remain.

The past holds wisdom we must seek,
In silent truths that softly speak.
In every tear, a promise shines,
In every loss, our spirit climbs.

Embrace the journey of the years,
In faith, we conquer all our fears.
The divine call rings ever true,
In yesteryears, we find the new.

Restoring the Spirit Within

In the quiet of the night,
We seek to shed the cloak of fright.
A journey deep within the soul,
To find the parts that make us whole.

With every prayer, a light does dawn,
A whisper soft, a gentle song.
In stillness, grace begins to flow,
Restoring peace where love will grow.

The burdens carried, laid to rest,
In faithful hands, we are blessed.
Forgiveness blooms like flowers fair,
Restoring joy in each heartfelt prayer.

As waters clear, so too our mind,
In sacred moments, truth we find.
The spirit dances, wild and free,
A testament of harmony.

So let us seek this sacred space,
Where love renews and fills with grace.
In every breath, the spirit sings,
Restoring life to all good things.

In the Lattice of the Universe

In the vastness where starlight weaves,
Whispers of creation gently breathe.
Each thread connects the heart of grace,
A tapestry of love in cosmic space.

Through the void, divine shadows dance,
Embracing souls in sacred trance.
Galaxies spin with purpose and might,
Illuminating truth in the dark of night.

In every atom, echoes of Him,
The universe sings a vibrant hymn.
We find our place, though small we seem,
Part of a vast and holy dream.

In the quiet of prayer, we touch the sky,
With hearts open wide, we learn to fly.
Guided by love in celestial grace,
We walk hand in hand with the stars we embrace.

The Mantle of My Truth

Beneath the folds of sacred light,
I seek the truth that feels so right.
Clothed in wisdom, the soul does shine,
In silence, we find the divine line.

The mantle wraps my weary frame,
A cloak of love, calling my name.
In trials faced and shadows cast,
I learn to rise from the storms of the past.

Each story shared, a thread of gold,
In the journey of life, brave and bold.
With faith as my guide, I walk with grace,
To find my truth in this sacred space.

In communion with all, I stand tall,
Through love, together, we shall not fall.
In every heart, the truth resides,
Embracing all, where beauty abides.

Echoes through Eternity's Gate

In the realms where silence speaks,
Time unveils what the spirit seeks.
Echoes rise through portals bright,
Whispered prayers take sacred flight.

Every heartbeat sings of peace,
A promise made, a sweet release.
Through the gate of dawn's embrace,
Divine echoes find their place.

In unity, our voices blend,
Each note a balm that seeks to mend.
Through trials faced and paths unknown,
We find the strength we've always sown.

Eternity's door swings wide and free,
To walk in love is to truly see.
With each step upon this earth,
We honor life and cherish worth.

Beneath the Wings of Creation

In the hush where the dawn takes flight,
Beneath the wings of purest light.
Creation breathes its gentle air,
A sigh of grace that whispers prayer.

Feathers woven in colors bold,
Stories of wisdom yet untold.
Each flap a promise, each glide a chance,
To rise above in a sacred dance.

Among the stars, where dreams reside,
We find our courage, hearts open wide.
In the solace of nature's song,
We learn the path where we belong.

In every heartbeat, love takes flight,
Guided by faith through day and night.
United beneath the sky's embrace,
We walk together in sacred space.

Chronicles of Quiet Reflection

In stillness, hearts align,
Seeking wisdom divine,
Amidst the whispers low,
Faith's gentle embers glow.

Beneath the vast expanse,
We ponder chance and grace,
Each moment softly speaks,
In silence, truth we seek.

The dawn breaks pure and clear,
Casting shadows of fear,
In prayer, our spirits rise,
Reaching for endless skies.

Through trials, we are led,
By light that never fades,
With humility we tread,
In the path that love made.

We gather in the peace,
Where all our doubts cease,
Embracing every tear,
As blessings draw us near.

The Labyrinth of Lost Years

In the maze of twilight dreams,
Time unfurls its gentle seams,
Every turn a lesson learned,
In the heart, a fire burned.

Whispers of the past reside,
In shadows where we bide,
Each memory a sacred stone,
In solitude, we've grown.

Through corridors of sighs,
Hope flickers, never dies,
With every step we've trod,
We find the face of God.

Footprints whisper ancient tales,
Of storms and peaceful gales,
In sorrow's tender clasp,
We learn to love, to gasp.

So onward through this night,
We chase the distant light,
For in each labyrinthine turn,
A brighter flame will burn.

Epiphanies from Silent Days

In quiet hours, wisdom speaks,
As sunlight on the peaks,
In moments still and kind,
We open up our mind.

When the world begins to fade,
And the noise, it does cascade,
In solitude we find peace,
As restless thoughts release.

Soft reflections, soft as dew,
Beneath the skies of blue,
In every gentle sigh,
We touch the sacred high.

In the hush, we hear the call,
Each heartbeat, echoing all,
In silence, grace descends,
An offering that mends.

Awakening the soul's delight,
In darkness, we find light,
With every still embrace,
We journey through His grace.

An Offering of Remembrance

With open hearts, we stand in prayer,
A tribute to the love we share,
In the echoes of the past,
We find our shadows cast.

Each memory a sacred thread,
In every tear that's shed,
We honor those who've gone,
In silence, they live on.

As candles flicker soft and bright,
Guiding us through the night,
Their laughter lingers still,
Within our hearts, they fill.

In every story told anew,
A piece of them shines through,
With every whispered name,
We kindle love's true flame.

Together we embrace the light,
In love's eternal flight,
Offering our hearts with grace,
In remembrance, time finds place.

The Spirit's Introspection

In silence deep, the soul does dwell,
A whisper soft, a sacred spell.
In contemplation's gentle fold,
Revealed are truths, both bright and bold.

The heart's eye opens, visions clear,
Unveiling paths that draw us near.
In stillness found, the light ascends,
A journey traced where love transcends.

The spirit's call, a beckoning sound,
In depths of faith, our hope is found.
With every breath, we seek the grace,
To find our home in love's embrace.

In shadows cast, our doubts arise,
Yet in the dark, His presence lies.
With every tear, a drop of light,
Transforming night into the bright.

We rise anew, like morning's hue,
Bathed in the warmth of skies so blue.
The spirit's flight, a tender guide,
In every heart, His love abides.

From Dust to Divine

From dust we rose, in breath of clay,
To seek the path, to find the way.
In sacred forms, the spirit weaves,
A tapestry of hope, and leaves.

With every step, the echo calls,
Through sacred halls where silence falls.
The promise held in whispered prayer,
Transcends the bounds of earthly care.

In fleeting hours, we dance with fate,
Embracing love, we learn to wait.
Each moment graced with holy light,
Transforms the dark, ignites the bright.

As stars above, our dreams take flight,
In faith we trust, in love we fight.
The journey longs for what's divine,
From dust to grace, our souls align.

In unity, our spirits soar,
Connected hearts forevermore.
From earthly binds, we seek to rise,
To heaven's doors, we lift our eyes.

Harbingers of the Inner Light

In morning's glow, the heart awakes,
To nurture hope, the spirit stakes.
As gentle whispers touch the soul,
We find our path, we reach our goal.

The harbinger, both near and far,
Guides seekers with a shining star.
Each lesson learned, each moment shared,
In love's embrace, we are prepared.

Through trials faced, our faith ignites,
Illuminating endless nights.
In darkest hours, a spark remains,
Where love prevails, where peace sustains.

The silent prayer, the heart's refrain,
Lifts every burden, heals all pain.
In every tear, a drop of grace,
We find our home, our sacred space.

With every soul's uplifting gaze,
We reflect His light in endless praise.
Together bound, our spirits dance,
In harmony, we take our chance.

The Scroll of True Existence

A scroll unfurls, in whispered tone,
The tale of life, the love alone.
In ink of faith, the stories lie,
Of countless souls who seek the why.

Each line a path, a journey shared,
With lessons learned, hearts truly bared.
Through trials faced, and battles fought,
In every moment, wisdom sought.

The pages turn, revealing light,
Glimmers of hope in darkest night.
With every tear, a lesson grows,
A testament to what love knows.

The scroll of life, in time unfolds,
In gentle strokes, our truth beholds.
A sacred dance, where faith and dreams,
Create a world that brightly beams.

From each beginning, joy expands,
In unity, we join our hands.
For in this scroll, a truth exists,
In every heart, His love persists.

In the Mirror of Grace

In the stillness of dawn's embrace,
I seek the reflection of Your grace.
A gentle whisper fills the air,
Reminding me You're always there.

With every breath, I find my way,
Led by the light of love each day.
Wounds of the past, though deep and wide,
Are healed in Your presence, where I abide.

In trials faced, I lift my eyes,
To the heavens, where mercy lies.
Casting fears into the sea,
In Your grace, I am set free.

From shadows long, I now depart,
Embracing joy within my heart.
For in Your mirror, truth unfolds,
A tapestry of love retold.

Let me walk the path You tread,
With every step, where angels led.
In the mirror of grace divine,
My soul finds peace, my heart aligned.

The Pilgrimage of the Heart

This journey leads where shadows play,
Through valleys low and mountains gray.
With faith as compass, love as guide,
In the pilgrimage, I will abide.

Each step I take, a prayer of sighs,
Beneath the vast and open skies.
I seek the truth in every mile,
In sacred silence, find Your smile.

With burdens light and spirit free,
In every heartache, I can see.
A glimmer of hope that never fades,
A testament, Your love invades.

Through storms that rage and tempests roar,
You hold my hand, I seek no more.
The burdens shared, together we rise,
A pilgrimage beneath Your skies.

In moments still, I hear the call,
A whisper sweet that guides us all.
The pilgrimage of heart and soul,
In faith and love, we become whole.

Casting Shadows of Yesterday

Upon the canvas of my mind,
Shadows linger, ties that bind.
Yet in the stillness, hope appears,
A promise bright that calms my fears.

Casting shadows, they melt away,
In Your light, I choose to stay.
Forgiveness blooms where pain once lay,
A new dawn rising, bright and gay.

The echoes of the past grow dim,
As I walk closer, hand in hand.
Your love a river, pure and wide,
In Your embrace, my heart will bide.

Though yesterday's scars may linger near,
Today's embrace wipes off the tear.
Each step a dance upon Your grace,
Transforming shadows into space.

A future bright, a hope reborn,
In faith I rise, with purpose sworn.
Casting shadows, I draw near,
In Your light, I know no fear.

A Covenant with My Soul

In sacred promise, I declare,
A covenant born from love and care.
With every heartbeat, I renew,
In trust profound, I follow You.

These vows I make, in quiet prayer,
Each moment cherished, pure and rare.
With You, my guide, I stand awake,
In every choice, my spirit's stake.

Through trials faced and joys bestowed,
In grace, I carry all my load.
Your light ignites what once was lost,
In every gain, I count the cost.

Together bound, my soul finds home,
In Your embrace, I'm never alone.
A covenant written, heart's own song,
In faith, I see where I belong.

With every tear, a lesson learned,
In love's reflection, I have yearned.
A sacred bond, forever whole,
This life, a gift, my covenant soul.

The Hymn of Lost Innocence

In the garden, shadows play,
Whispers of what lost the day.
Tender roots of childhood's grace,
Faded echoes, they leave no trace.

Morning light, a stranger's face,
Yearns for warmth in empty space.
Tears like beads upon the floor,
Lost in dreams, forevermore.

Once, the laughter filled the air,
Now mere silence, none to share.
The melodies of joy now fade,
Innocence, a debt we paid.

Gentle hands that soothed the night,
Now are ghosts, no hope in sight.
Yet in prayer, we seek to find,
Healing grace for troubled mind.

In sacred soil where sorrows grow,
Seeds of wisdom start to show.
Through the pain, we rise and stand,
Lost, yet finding the divine hand.

Celestial Reflections of the Self

In the mirror of the night,
Stars ignite our inner light.
Casting shadows on the ground,
In their glow, our truths are found.

Waves of time, they ebb and flow,
Guiding hearts where journey goes.
Constellations whisper dreams,
In their dance, our spirit beams.

Every heartbeat calls the wise,
Echoed in the boundless skies.
Fragments of our soul's embrace,
Shining bright in endless space.

Life's reflections intertwined,
Body, spirit, ever aligned.
In the silence, answers dwell,
Celestial tales, we weave and tell.

So, in prayer, our voices rise,
Shooting stars and whispered sighs.
Wonders found in every breath,
Life eternal, beyond death.

Treading the Path of Memory

Footsteps trace the sands of time,
Whispers caught in ancient rhyme.
Every moment, precious spark,
Guiding through the endless dark.

In twilight's hold, reflections weave,
Stories told of those we grieve.
In the silence, memories bloom,
Filling hearts with love's sweet tune.

Echoes of a child's soft laugh,
Marking joy upon the path.
In the stillness, footprints show,
Lessons learned where sorrows grow.

Journey forward, yet look back,
Find the strength, regain what's lack.
Each sorrow weighed, a treasure too,
In the dark, light breaks anew.

Hand in hand with past, we stride,
Glimmers of hope, our faithful guide.
In remembrance, love will reign,
Through the joy and through the pain.

Ethereal Conversations with the Past

In the twilight, shadows call,
Voices echo through the hall.
Softly, secrets drift like smoke,
Words of wisdom, softly spoke.

The past dances, calls my name,
Memory's spark, an endless flame.
Through the veil, I hear the sound,
Of love and loss, forever bound.

In the quiet, hearts converse,
Time unfolds its sacred verse.
With every sigh, a lesson learned,
In every tear, the past returned.

Whispers shared beneath the stars,
Tales of life, our hidden scars.
Ethereal threads from soul to soul,
In their weave, we find our whole.

In dusk's embrace, we find the truth,
Sacred ties to every youth.
In each moment we release,
Past and present find their peace.

Chasing the Light of the Unseen

In shadows deep, we seek the glow,
A whisper soft, where spirits flow.
Beyond the veil, where truth abides,
We chase the light that never hides.

With faith as our guide, we wander wide,
In the silence, the heart's true guide.
Through trials faced, our souls will rise,
Towards the dawn of endless skies.

In moments still, the light appears,
As hope ignites, dissolving fears.
We reach for grace, in every breath,
Embracing life, even in death.

The unseen light, our sacred quest,
A beacon bright, within our chest.
We'll walk together, hand in hand,
On paths of love, in this holy land.

Resurrecting the Spirit

From ashes rise, the spirit fights,
In quietude, it finds its sights.
Awakening from slumber deep,
To guard the hope we strive to keep.

In shadows cast, where doubt may dwell,
The heart proclaims a sacred spell.
With every breath, the past will fade,
New life emerges, unafraid.

Through trials faced, our spirits soar,
In love's embrace, forevermore.
Each heartbeat sings a wayward hymn,
As dawn unveils, the light within.

Together we stand, in fervent prayer,
Resurrecting dreams from despair.
With open hearts, the spirit glows,
In every soul, divine love flows.

In the Garden of Forgotten Selves

In the garden where shadows play,
The lost ones linger, night and day.
Among the blooms, their whispers sigh,
As memories fade, yet hope still flies.

Beneath the trees, old echoes hum,
Life's tender roots, where we come from.
In silent grace, we seek to mend,
The threads of time that will not end.

Tender hearts can find their way,
Through hidden paths where sorrows lay.
The blossoms speak of paths once tread,
As light awakens the dreams once dead.

In every petal, a soul's refrain,
The garden holds both joy and pain.
Embrace the past, let shadows part,
In the forgotten, we find our heart.

Clarity in the Divine Mirror

In the mirror, reflections gleam,
Piercing through the waking dream.
Each transient face, a story told,
In the depths, our spirits unfold.

With every gaze, the heart takes flight,
Discovering truths cloaked in light.
Mirrored souls, a sacred bond,
Seeking wisdom, we wander beyond.

In clarity found, our fears subside,
As love ignites, we do abide.
The echo of grace, the silent call,
In each reflection, we find it all.

Through the glass, we see the divine,
Our journey weaves, in sacred line.
With open eyes, we choose to see,
The truth in love's infinity.

The Ascendance of Forgotten Hopes

In the silence of the night,
Whispers of dreams take flight.
Hearts once heavy now arise,
Guided by the starlit skies.

Echoes of the prayers we shared,
In shadows deep, we were ensnared.
Yet faith ignites a brighter spark,
Lifting souls from sorrow's dark.

Cast aside the fears we wore,
With each breath, we'll seek the shore.
In unity, our voices soar,
Together, we will seek for more.

Hope's embrace, a gentle tide,
In its warmth, we shall abide.
From ashes, we will rise anew,
Clothed in love, the path is true.

So let the dawn of promise break,
With every step, the chains will shake.
The ascendance of our rightful place,
In His light, we find our grace.

Celestial Footprints in Time

Upon the sands of fleeting days,
Celestial footprints guide our ways.
Each step a story etched in gold,
In mysteries of heavens bold.

When shadows cloak the path we tread,
Look close, and faith will be our thread.
For every tear, a star will shine,
Reminding us, we are divine.

Through ages, love has stood the test,
In trials, we are truly blessed.
The heavens whisper secrets vast,
As we journey forth, our fears surpassed.

Time holds our hearts in gentle hands,
In all we do, His will still stands.
With every heartbeat, let us sing,
Of hope restored, of blessings spring.

In gratitude, we mark the days,
With every breath, we share His praise.
Celestial footprints, clear and bright,
Illuminate our path with light.

The Essence I Left Behind

In shadows deep, my whispers fade,
Yet in each heart, my love is laid.
The essence lingers, sweet and pure,
In every thought, a love so sure.

Through trials faced and storms endured,
My silent watch, forever assured.
In laughter shared, and tears we shed,
The essence lives, though I am dead.

With every life I've touched and changed,
In memories, our souls exchanged.
The beauty found in fleeting glance,
In every moment, life's great dance.

Though time may steal, the heart remains,
In every joy, and every pain.
The essence whispers, ever nigh,
A testament that love won't die.

So when you feel the gentle breeze,
Know I am there, among the trees.
The essence I left behind shall stay,
A love eternal, come what may.

Chants of Resurrection

In sacred space, the echoes ring,
Chants of hope, our spirits sing.
From depths of sorrow, we arise,
Through faith renewed, we touch the skies.

With every note, the heart takes flight,
Transforming darkness into light.
In unity, our voices blend,
A symphony that knows no end.

The pulse of life beats strong and true,
In every soul, a spark renewed.
From ashes, beauty comes to be,
Through wounds, we find our harmony.

As petals open to the morn,
Embrace the promise of reborn.
With every dawn, a chance to rise,
Through chants of resurrection, we realize.

So let us gather, hand in hand,
In joyful songs, we make our stand.
For life, a gift, forever shared,
In chants of love, our hearts are bared.

The Tides of Divine Memory

In the stillness of dawn, I seek,
The echoes of grace that softly speak.
Waves of faith on shores of time,
Carving paths through the sacred rhyme.

Beneath the heavens, whispers soar,
Guiding souls to the open door.
With every tide, a story unfolds,
Of mercy and love, eternally told.

In shadows cast by fleeting day,
Resilience shines in sacred play.
Each moment gathered, a holy thread,
Binding the living with those long dead.

With every heartbeat, truth I find,
In the dance of spirit, loving and kind.
The tides recede, revealing each stone,
Beneath the deep, we are never alone.

So let the waters rise and fall,
For in this rhythm, I hear the call.
A tide of memory, pure and bright,
Guides me home to eternal light.

Echoes of My Former Light

In the chamber of my heart, I yearn,
Echoes rise, like candles that burn.
Reflections of joy, shadows of pain,
Whispers of wisdom, like gentle rain.

Once a beacon, bright and free,
I wandered far, lost at sea.
Yet through the fog, a glimmer remained,
Threads of the past in the soul, ingrained.

Through valleys deep, I've learned to tread,
Following whispers of the light I fed.
Every step, a prayer, every breath, a song,
In the tapestry of life, I belong.

As dawn breaks the horizon wide,
I gather the echoes, casting aside.
Illumined paths now call to me,
In the silence, I find the key.

So with grace, I rise to embrace,
The echoes of light in this sacred space.
In the heart's quiet, I long to see,
The divine reflection that sets me free.

The Sanctuary of Self-Discovery

Within the depths of silence profound,
A sanctuary waits, where grace is found.
Each whisper sings of truths untold,
In the heart's chamber, gems unfold.

In the stillness, I turn within,
Awakening the strength that has always been.
Softly, shadows begin to fade,
Illuminating the dreams I've made.

The journey inward, a sacred quest,
Seeking the essence, I am blessed.
With every breath, a blessing shared,
In the tapestry of life, I've dared.

Among the echoes of the past,
I find the courage, a soul steadfast.
With each revelation, I rise anew,
In the sanctuary, I embrace the true.

So, gently I weave the threads of grace,
In the stillness, I find my place.
For in this haven, my spirit flies,
A sanctuary where my soul complies.

Whispered Prayers to the Past

In the twilight's glow, I softly pray,
Whispers of hope from yesterday.
Carried on winds of sweet refrain,
I seek the lessons nestled in pain.

Ancestors' voices kiss the air,
Guiding my heart with tender care.
In shadows long, their wisdom shines,
Through trials faced, I find the signs.

With each prayer, a thread I weave,
Ties to the past, a gift to receive.
Moments linger, like stars in night,
Illuminating the path to light.

So let me honor the journey made,
In gratitude, I am unafraid.
With every whisper, a bond renewed,
In the tapestry of life, I am imbued.

In reverence, I send my prayer,
To the past that shaped me, a love laid bare.
For in their embrace, I rise and stand,
Whispered prayers, my heart in hand.

The Rustic Altar of Youth

In fields where laughter softly plays,
The sun bestows its golden rays.
We gather dreams upon the earth,
At this altar, we find our worth.

With hands of clay and hearts so pure,
We build our hopes, a faith secure.
Each moment shared, a timeless gift,
In love's embrace, our spirits lift.

The trees around us whisper low,
Of secrets held where wildflowers grow.
Each petal soft, a prayer unspoken,
In youth's sweet garden, hope's not broken.

As twilight falls, the stars ignite,
A symphony of purest light.
We dance together, side by side,
In youth's embrace, we shall abide.

Forgive the past, with all its fears,
For in these moments, joy appears.
At the rustic altar of our days,
We find our faith in simple ways.

The Graceful Return

Through valleys deep, and mountains high,
I seek the truth beneath the sky.
With every step, my soul does yearn,
For love's embrace, the graceful return.

Each path I walk, a lesson learned,
In every heart, a fire burned.
A journey long, through joy and strife,
I find the light, the gift of life.

Upon the breeze, the whispers call,
Of hope and faith that never fall.
In silence sweet, your spirit speaks,
In sacred moments, love's heart seeks.

As days unfold, and seasons change,
In nature's dance, I feel so strange.
Yet every tear that I have shed,
Brings forth the blooms of grace instead.

When shadows loom, and doubt appears,
I bow my head and quell my fears.
For every end leads to the start,
In graceful return, I find my heart.

My Heart's Sacred Archive

Within my chest, a sacred space,
Where love and sorrow, time can't erase.
Each memory a treasured song,
In my heart's archive, I belong.

The laughter shared, the tears we weep,
In every moment, memories keep.
A tapestry of joy and pain,
In sacred corners, love remains.

The pages turn with every breath,
Each story woven, life and death.
In quiet nights, when shadows play,
My heart recalls the light of day.

In gentle whispers, truth unfolds,
Of dreams once bright and futures bold.
My heart, a keeper of the light,
Preserves each spark of pure delight.

With reverence, I guard these ties,
In every glance, a world of sighs.
In life's embrace, I find my way,
My heart's archive shall ever stay.

The Passage of Light Through Time

In ancient woods, where shadows dwell,
A tale of light begins to swell.
Through ages past, the whispers flow,
As time reveals what we must know.

Each ray that pierces through the dusk,
Awakens faith, ignites the trust.
In morning's glow, new hope will rise,
A fleeting glimpse of boundless skies.

The stars above, a guiding hand,
In firm embrace, our fears disband.
For every moment, swift and bright,
Is but a step towards the light.

Through winding paths, the journey calls,
A symphony of rise and falls.
We walk in grace, our spirits soar,
In the passage of light, forevermore.

With every dawn, the shadows fade,
A promise kept, a prayer made.
In time's embrace, we find our way,
The passage of light, our souls' ballet.

Echoes of the Soul's Pilgrimage

Through valleys deep, I find my way,
Each whisper guides, a gentle sway.
The stars above, they softly gleam,
In prayerful silence, I dare to dream.

The path is worn by feet of grace,
In every step, I seek His face.
With every heartbeat, a sacred vow,
Led by His light, I stand here now.

Mountains rise, a steadfast call,
In shadows cast, I rise, not fall.
The river flows, my burdens cease,
With faith as my boat, I find my peace.

The echoes ring of saints long past,
In their whispers, my fears contrast.
I lift my voice in hymns divine,
With every note, my heart aligns.

Beneath the sun, my spirit soars,
In love unbound, my soul explores.
Through trials faced, in grace I stand,
Forever seeking that holy land.

Sanctum of My Reflection

In stillness found, a sacred space,
I gaze within, a holy grace.
The mirror holds my deepest fears,
Yet through the glass, love's light appears.

Each breath I take is laced with prayer,
In this retreat, I shed my care.
The whispers soft, they call my name,
In silence loud, I feel the flame.

Upon the altar of my heart,
I lay my burdens, each part.
The sacred trust, a bond so pure,
In faith I stand, my soul secure.

The echoes dance in twilight's glow,
In every shadow, love will grow.
With gratitude, I lift my plea,
In hushed reverence, I am free.

The sanctum bright, a cherished space,
Where shadows fade and light takes place.
With open eyes, I see it clear,
This sacred ground, forever near.

In the Shadow of Seraphim

In the realm where angels dwell,
Their wings like whispers weave a spell.
I walk beneath their watchful gaze,
In quiet awe, my spirit stays.

The light cascades, a heavenly stream,
I lift my heart, my soul's redeem.
With every flutter, hope ignites,
In the embrace of sacred heights.

The seraphim, their songs resound,
In harmony, I am unbound.
Through trials faced and joys unfurled,
I find my place within this world.

Their shadows cast, a gentle shield,
In faith's embrace, I am revealed.
With every breath, I feel their grace,
In holy presence, I find my place.

Through every storm, their wings will guide,
In the embrace of love, abide.
Beneath the stars, my spirit sings,
In the shadow, joy forever springs.

The Unearthed Identity

In quiet moments, truth unfolds,
The essence found in tales retold.
With the dawn, the shadows flee,
I rise anew, a soul set free.

Each layer shed reveals the core,
In sacred light, I am restored.
The past remains, yet does not bind,
In every heartbeat, love I find.

The script of life, I now embrace,
Within my heart, a sacred space.
With open hands, I take my stand,
In this journey, guided by His hand.

Awakening, I claim my name,
In every trial, I find the same.
The journey's end is but the start,
This unearthed truth shall never part.

In every tear, a lesson learned,
The fire of faith forever burned.
With every sunrise, I shall rise,
In the embrace of love, the prize.

Gospel of the Unremembered

In shadows deep, the whispers fade,
A story lost, in silence laid.
Voices call from realms unseen,
Awakening the souls between.

Through ancient paths, we wander bare,
Seeking truth in the still air.
Each echo tells a tale of grace,
In the heart's quiet, sacred space.

The light of hope shines ever bright,
Guiding us through the darkest night.
With open hearts, we seek the light,
In the love that meets our plight.

For all the dreams that fade away,
A promise held, come what may.
In the unremembered, we find peace,
And from our sorrows, sweet release.

So let us gather, hand in hand,
In this journey across the land.
Together, we'll revive the songs,
Of the timeless love where we belong.

The Sacred Echoes of Time

In the stillness of the morn,
Sacred echo, softly borne.
Every heartbeat sings a prayer,
Reaching out into the air.

From the dawn's first gleam, we rise,
Looking deep into the skies.
Time unveils its sacred path,
In the midst of love's sweet wrath.

Ancient wisdom guides our way,
As we walk, we learn to pray.
Each step made in trust divine,
Brings us closer, heart to shrine.

Veils of doubt may cloud our sight,
Yet in darkness, there is light.
With each echo, we reclaim,
The sacred whispers of His name.

Through the ages, we find grace,
In the warmth of love's embrace.
The sacred echoes, soft and true,
Remind us all, we are made new.

The Communion of Forgotten Dreams

In twilight realms, dreams softly fade,
Yet in our hearts, they've often stayed.
Through whispered prayers, we find our way,
In the communion of each day.

The seeds of hope in silence grow,
In gentle winds, their blessings flow.
Each forgotten dream a thread,
In the tapestry of love we've spread.

We gather 'neath the starry night,
In shared visions of the light.
Through open hearts, we join as one,
In the midst of all we've won.

With every tear, a joy reborn,
From brokenness, the heart is torn.
Yet in each piece, we're made complete,
In the harmony where we meet.

Let us linger, let us share,
In the love that binds us there.
For every dream that slips away,
In God's embrace, we learn to stay.

The Pilgrim's Prayer for the Lost

As pilgrims on this winding road,
We carry hearts, we bear the load.
To those who wander, lost and weary,
We send a prayer, both light and cheery.

With open hands, we seek to serve,
In love and grace, our hearts preserve.
For every soul that slips from sight,
We gather hope, we share the light.

Through trials faced, we learn to stand,
And walk with faith, hand in hand.
To guide the lost, we shall arise,
As beacons 'neath the endless skies.

Each tear we've wept, a sacred flame,
With every breath, we call their name.
To the forsaken, we extend,
The warmth of love, a true friend.

So let our voices rise in song,
In every note, where we belong.
The pilgrim's prayer is never lost,
In love's embrace, we count the cost.

The Covenant of Self

In the stillness of my heart, I seek,
A whisper of light, gentle and meek.
A promise made, a bond so true,
In every breath, I start anew.

With every dawn, I rise and find,
In shadows deep, Your grace entwined.
The mirror reflects the soul's pure light,
Guiding me forth, through day and night.

In silence, I hear the sacred call,
In laughter and tears, I give my all.
Together we walk this path of trust,
In faith, I stand, in love, I must.

Through trials faced and battles won,
I forge my faith, just like the sun.
In every choice, Your hand I see,
Transforming my spirit, setting it free.

The journey inward, vast and wide,
With every step, You're by my side.
The covenant of self eternally binds,
A promise of peace, where love unwinds.

Pilgrim's Reverie

I wander through valleys serene and bright,
Each step beckons, drawn by the light.
The path unfolds beneath my feet,
In sacred whispers, life's heartbeat.

With every hill, a story told,
Of faith unyielding, a spirit bold.
The skies reflect hopes, dreams unchained,
A pilgrim's heart, through joy and pain.

Temptations rise, like shadows creep,
Yet in my soul, the promise I keep.
For every struggle sharpens the sword,
In humble prayer, I hold the Lord.

Stars above guide my sight,
In the darkness, Your love ignites.
With open heart, I walk this land,
Each step a prayer, each moment planned.

As dawn breaks, hope's colors blend,
I find my journey has no end.
A reverie of faith, forever true,
In every heartbeat, I dwell in You.

Beneath the Stars

Beneath the stars, I lay my head,
In night's embrace, my spirit spread.
The universe hums a soothing tune,
In Your presence, I am immune.

The cosmos sparkles with divine grace,
Each twinkling light, a sacred place.
I whisper secrets to the night air,
Under the heavens, I cast my prayer.

The moon, so bright, watches near,
Guiding lost souls, calms every fear.
In this moment, I find my way,
Reflecting on dreams of a brighter day.

The whispers of angels intertwine,
In shimmering silence, I see the sign.
Each heartbeat echoes the cosmic song,
In the peace of the night, I belong.

With open arms, I embrace the night,
In the tapestry woven from purest light.
Beneath the stars, I feel the bind,
A brilliant love transcending time.

I Found

In the quiet corners of despair,
I found a hope that filled the air.
A light that flickers in darkest night,
A gentle voice, the soul's delight.

Through thickened fog and shadowed ways,
I wandered lost for countless days.
Yet in the depths of silence grand,
I found the touch of Your loving hand.

The storms may rage, the winds may blow,
Yet in Your arms, I'm free to grow.
A refuge strong, a heart so pure,
In trials faced, Your love is sure.

I found the strength to rise anew,
In every tear, the sky shines blue.
The journey long, but now I see,
That through it all, You walked with me.

In every heartbeat, I am found,
In every prayer, love knows no bound.
With gratitude, my spirit sings,
I found my peace in all that clings.

The Tapestry of My Sacred Journey

Each thread woven, a story unfolds,
Of trials faced and treasures gold.
In the fabric of faith, I'm stitched tight,
A masterpiece shaped in love's pure light.

The colors dance with vibrant hue,
Each moment precious, each heartbeat true.
Lessons learned in laughter and pain,
In every loss, I find love's gain.

The hands of time craft and mold,
A sacred journey, each step behold.
In faith's embrace, I choose to soar,
With wings of grace, forevermore.

Within this tapestry, I see the line,
Of lives intertwined, a grand design.
In unity's weave, together we grow,
Sharing the love that we both know.

As I look back, my heart takes flight,
In every struggle, there's unwavering light.
The tapestry glows, a sacred guide,
In every moment, You are my pride.

The Altar of Abandonment

At the altar I lay my fears,
In silence I shed my tears.
With open heart, I release the bind,
In surrender, true peace I find.

The weight of the past, I willingly give,
In this moment, I truly live.
Divine hands cradle my soul's plea,
In abandonment, I am set free.

Echoes of doubt fade into the night,
In the stillness, I find my light.
Whispers of faith weave through the air,
At this altar, my burdens lay bare.

A sacred vow to let go and trust,
In God's grace, I am filled with lust.
The path ahead shines brilliantly bright,
At this altar, I embrace the light.

With every tear, a seed is sown,
In fertile ground, my spirit has grown.
A journey of love, of faith, and grace,
At the altar, I find my place.

Beneath the Canopy of Grace

Beneath the trees where shadows dance,
I linger here in a holy trance.
The leaves whisper prayers, soft and low,
In this sacred space, my spirit shall grow.

The sunlight filters through branches wide,
In warmth and peace, I shall abide.
Each rustle of wind speaks truth to me,
Beneath this canopy, my heart is free.

I gather the blessings that softly fall,
In gratitude, I cherish them all.
With every breath, I breathe in the grace,
A divine embrace in this holy place.

The earth beneath, a steadfast home,
In nature's arms, I shall not roam.
Each moment here, a gift from above,
Beneath the canopy, I learn of love.

So let the heavens and earth combine,
In this union, my heart shall shine.
With faith as my guide, I walk this space,
Forever sheltered beneath grace.

A Revelation in Stillness

In stillness, the world fades away,
All thoughts and worries, I gently sway.
Here in the quiet, I find divine,
A revelation, pure and fine.

The universe whispers secrets untold,
In moments of hush, the truth unfolds.
With every heartbeat, I hear the call,
In the depths of silence, I find it all.

The soul's journey unfolds in peace,
Where noise and chaos tend to cease.
In the calm, I sense His grace,
A revelation, a holy space.

Awakening blooms within my chest,
In stillness, I feel eternally blessed.
A dance with the heavens in soft embrace,
In silence, I find my rightful place.

With each breath drawn, a deeper sigh,
In sacred stillness, I learn to fly.
A revelation gifted by the divine,
In the quietude, my spirit aligns.

The Beatitudes of My Being

Blessed are the meek, for they shall rise,
With gentle hearts, they touch the skies.
In kindness, they walk the humble path,
In love's embrace, they find God's wrath.

Blessed are those who mourn and weep,
Their sorrow, a treasure they shall keep.
In the depths of grief, joy will bloom,
Through lessons learned in darkest room.

Blessed are the pure in heart, they see,
The beauty of faith that sets us free.
In clear reflections, God's light shines bright,
In their innocence, they hold the right.

Blessed are the seekers of peace and grace,
In their endeavor, they find their space.
With open arms, they gather all,
In harmony's echo, they stand tall.

Blessed are those called to live in love,
With every action, they rise above.
In the beatitudes, we find our song,
In unity, we shall all belong.

The Divine Tapestry of Memory

In threads of time, His mercy weaves,
Each moment a stitch in our hearts' eaves.
A tapestry bright with love's embrace,
Guiding our souls in the sacred space.

Memories pulse like stars in the night,
Flashing reminders of grace and light.
Each joy and sorrow, a lesson learned,
In the fabric of faith, our spirits burned.

We gather the shards of hopes once lost,
Reviving the dreams, no matter the cost.
His whispers guide us through pain and strife,
In the woven moments, we find our life.

A dance of shadows, we twirl and fly,
Embracing the truth that will never die.
With every thread, a story we tell,
In the sacred weave, we find all is well.

With each passing stitch, the world grows clear,
The threads of His mercy draw ever near.
In the Echoes of Him, we stand united,
In the Divine tapestry, our souls ignited.

A Faith Reclaimed

From ashes of doubt, a flame ignites,
With fervent hearts embracing the sights.
A journey renewed on pathways of grace,
In the arms of Belief, we find our place.

Chains that once held us now gently break,
With courage and love, we rise for His sake.
In shadows of fear, His light we reclaim,
A whisper of hope, forever the same.

With every prayer lifted, our spirits soar,
In the quiet moments, we seek and implore.
The echoes of faith like a soothing balm,
Restore our hearts and keep them calm.

Every trial endured, a testament true,
To the power of love that guides us through.
In unity forged, our voices resound,
With a faith reclaimed, our strengths unbound.

Together we walk on this hallowed ground,
In the arms of the Father, forever found.
With hands lifted high, our praises we bring,
In the song of the soul, let His glory sing.

The Sacrifice of Self

In the quiet moments, surrender unfolds,
The sacrifice offered, a story retold.
With hearts bared open, we navigate pain,
In giving of self, our souls we gain.

The burdens we carry, they weigh like stone,
Yet in His presence, we are never alone.
For in letting go, we embrace the light,
Through shadows of darkness, our faith takes flight.

With every act rendered, love's seeds we sow,
Through sacrifice shared, the garden will grow.
Each challenge a stepping stone on the path,
To a deeper communion, beyond all wrath.

In the echoes of service, our spirits unite,
Each life a mirror reflecting the light.
For in losing our hold, we truly find peace,
In the sacrifice of self, our troubles cease.

Together we gather, in humility's grace,
In the journey of love, we all have a place.
With open hearts, we offer our best,
In the sacrifice of self, we find our rest.

Parables of What Once Was

In stories of old, the wisdom we glean,
Parables whispered, where hearts have been.
Lessons of love, of loss and of grace,
In the echoes of time, we find our trace.

Once, in the gardens where shadows grew long,
A tale of redemption, a sorrowful song.
With every trial faced, a truth we embrace,
In the chapters of life, we find our place.

The echoes of laughter, the sighs of despair,
Are woven together in love's tender care.
Through the light and the dark, our spirits entwined,
In the parables told, our hearts are aligned.

From mountains so lofty to valleys so deep,
The stories we carry, in silence we keep.
In each faded page, the echoes of grace,
In the spirit of love, we find our space.

Let the tales remind us of journeys we've traveled,
In the threads of our lives, all conflicts unraveled.
Through parables shared, we ignite the spark,
In the wisdom of ages, we light up the dark.

The Echoing Blessings of Old

In silence, ancient whispers flow,
Carried by winds that gently blow.
Each word a treasure, softly shared,
In hearts entwined, faith declared.

Through trials faced, the spirit grows,
With every path, the wisdom shows.
The light of ages, ever near,
In each echo, a voice sincere.

The moonlit night and sunlit dawn,
Remind us of the love we've drawn.
From times of yore, to present day,
In prayerful hearts, the blessings stay.

The stories told in sacred space,
Reveal the beauty of His grace.
Each moment treasured in our souls,
In unity, our spirit rolls.

So let us walk the path with trust,
In every challenge, rise we must.
For in the blessings that we seek,
The echoing truths shall never speak.

Reverent Reflections on What Was

Upon the altar of my mind,
The moments past, I seek to find.
In shadows cast, the lessons glow,
As angels whisper soft and low.

The trials faced, a sacred gift,
In every hardship, spirits lift.
The tapestry of love and pain,
Weaves a strength that shall remain.

In reverence, the memories rise,
Like dawn's light in the endless skies.
The echoes of a distant song,
In harmony, we all belong.

Each lesson learned, an ode to grace,
In every stumble, a warm embrace.
We gather strength from those before,
In gratitude, we seek to soar.

Let wisdom guide our tender hearts,
As from the past, a new life starts.
In reverent peace, we make our way,
Towards a brighter, holy day.

Finding God in My Past

In years gone by, I sought His face,
In every moment, felt His grace.
Through joy and sorrow, He was there,
A gentle whisper, love to share.

In childhood dreams and youthful fights,
In darkest days, and brightest nights.
Each step I took, God walked beside,
A faithful friend, my heart's guide.

The laughter shared, the tears that fell,
In every story, He made me dwell.
In trials faced, I found my way,
Through faith renewed, I learn to pray.

With every dawn, His mercies rise,
In grateful hearts, each moment lies.
The love I found in days of yore,
Shall lead me back to Him once more.

For in the past, the truth unfolds,
A gentle hand that softly holds.
In every heartbeat, every breath,
I find my God, even in death.

The Guardian of My Inner Truth

In stillness, I feel the sacred space,
Where whispers guide with gentle grace.
The guardian within, my soul's delight,
In shadows deep, she brings forth light.

With courage drawn from ancient lore,
She teaches me to seek for more.
In every challenge, strength is found,
A sacred bond that knows no bound.

Through storms that rage and skies so clear,
Her watchful eye, forever near.
In quiet moments, she reveals,
The depths of truth, the heart that heals.

With every prayer, I find my voice,
In loving grace, I make my choice.
To walk the path that leads to light,
With faith as armor, day and night.

So may I honor this holy guide,
In every struggle, by my side.
For in her gaze, I learn to see,
The guardian of my truth set free.

Through the Veil of Childhood

In the dawn of innocence's glow,
Laughter dances like a breeze,
Each moment a sacred story,
In the heart, a tranquil ease.

Soft whispers of forgotten dreams,
Children's eyes, a mirror bright,
Guided by the hand of grace,
Through shadows, into light.

The world dressed in vibrant hues,
Pure joy, a humble prayer,
Every step, a holy walk,
With echoes of care.

Tender hearts, with spirits free,
In play, they learn to find,
The beauty woven in the now,
A truth that's unconfined.

So let us learn from their first steps,
In each giggle, sweet and clear,
Life's essence in their laughter,
A melody we hold dear.

Serenity in the Fragments

In broken pieces, we find peace,
Shattered dreams, yet hope prevails,
Each crack a testament of grace,
In silence, a spirit hails.

The gentle touch of morning light,
Illuminates the paths we tread,
In every shadow, a whisper calls,
Guiding hearts where angels led.

Embracing flaws, the human soul,
With every scar a story told,
In the tapestry of life we weave,
Fractured threads turn into gold.

Find the sacred in the fall,
Lift the veil of doubt and fear,
In every fragment, love remains,
A song that rings so clear.

Serenity unfolds in time,
In chaos, peace entwined,
Through brokenness, we are made whole,
In unity, our hearts aligned.

A Testament of Inner Light

Within the depths, the light does dwell,
A flicker in the darkened night,
Each soul ignites a sacred spark,
A testament of inner light.

In quietude, the whispers speak,
Guiding stars bright in the sky,
A journey through the vast unknown,
With faith, we learn to fly.

Each heartbeat holds a sacred truth,
In stillness, strength is found,
The light within, a beacon bright,
In love, we're tightly bound.

Embrace the essence that you are,
Let kindness pave your way,
In every act, a ripple grows,
Reflecting light of day.

Together, we shine in harmony,
Casting shadows far and wide,
In unity, the world becomes,
A canvas where we abide.

The Resounding Silence of Eternity

In silence lies the secret world,
Where time stands still, and thoughts transcend,
A realm of whispers, soft and pure,
Here, all beginnings blend with ends.

The echoes of an ancient song,
Resound within the depths of grace,
In every breath, a pulse of life,
In stillness, we find our place.

Through the fabric of each heartbeat,
The cosmos unfolds its might,
In the pause between our words,
Infinity takes flight.

Each moment, a reflection deep,
In quietude, we seek the whole,
The lessons woven in this hush,
Unravel the threads of the soul.

In the space between the stars,
Eternity whispers near,
In the resounding silence held,
We find the love we hold dear.

Milton Keynes UK
Ingram Content Group UK Ltd.
UKHW020039271124
451585UK00012B/952